CON

A Mirror publication
Head of Syndication & Licensing: Fergus McKenna
Mirrorpix: David Scripps
020 7293 3858

Produced by Trinity Mirror Media
PO BOX 48, Liverpool L69 3EB
ISBN 9781907324215

Executive Editor: Ken Rogers
Senior Editor: Steve Hanrahan
Senior Art Editor: Rick Cooke
Editor: Paul Dove
Compiled by: Vicky Andrews
Designers: Vicky Andrews, Colin Harrison, Zoe Bevan

Part of the Mirror Collection
© Published by Trinity Mirror 2012
Images: Mirrorpix, PA Photos, Trinity Mirror
Printed by William Gibbons

A GLORIOUS 60 YEARS

An important piece of British history is made in 2012 with The Queen reaching 60 years on the throne, the second-longest reign in history.

Queen Elizabeth (the Queen Mother) with her daughter Princess Elizabeth on the balcony of Buckingham Palace, after the Coronation of King George VI in 1937

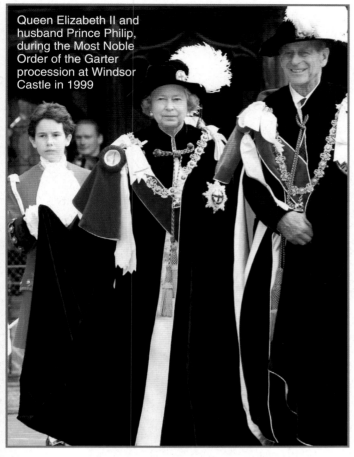

Queen Elizabeth II and husband Prince Philip, during the Most Noble Order of the Garter procession at Windsor Castle in 1999

THE Queen is characteristically gracious in stressing how touched she is by the support of the British people. Equally we, the British people, are fortunate to have a monarch we can admire in turbulent, uncertain times.

She has been a rock of dignity and wisdom, setting an example as the mother of the nation. No wonder other countries are envious of our Queen.

For Her Majesty, February 6, 1952, denotes the very beginning of her reign, but it is also a day tinged with sadness as the anniversary of the death of her father, King George VI. She has served him and us superbly, reigning magnificently for 60 years.

And we look forward to the many more years to come. She has put duty first each and every day of her reign.

This year was no exception as the Queen marked her historic Diamond Jubilee with public engagements and revealed in a special message how touched she has been by the British people.

She said: "As I mark 60 years as your Queen, I am writing to thank you for the wonderful support and encouragement that you have given to me and Prince Philip over these years and to tell you how deeply moved we have been to receive so many kind messages about the Diamond Jubilee.

"In this special year, as I dedicate myself anew to your service, I hope that we will all be reminded of the power of togetherness and ➤

Crowds in The Mall, London, during the Queen's Golden Jubilee celebrations in 2002

The Queen meets Canon Marcus Knight at St Paul's Cathedral in 1955

Queen Elizabeth II and the Duke of Edinburgh in the Grand Entrance at Buckingham Palace in 1953. The Duke is wearing the uniform of the Admiral of the Fleet

SOVEREIGN SMILE

Above, Queen Elizabeth leaves
Westminister Abbey after the
rehearsal for the Coronation of 1953.
The Duke of Norfolk shakes hands
with the Duke of Edinburgh. Left,
the Queen and Princess Anne take
baby Prince Andrew for a ride in his
high pram in the grounds of Balmoral
Castle on his first holiday in 1960

the convening strength of family, friendship and good neighbourliness, examples of which I have been fortunate to see throughout my reign and which my family and I look forward to seeing in many forms as we travel throughout the UK and the wider Commonwealth."

Her Majesty celebrates her 86th birthday this year, and while the nation she inherited is almost unrecognisable – after 12 Prime Ministers, four recessions and a technological revolution – she has remained a constant figure at its helm.

As the head of a Commonwealth of two billion people in 54 countries, and with a staff of 800 in her opulent main home of Buckingham Palace alone, she is surrounded by luxury.

But despite being worth an estimated £250million, the Queen enjoys life's simple pleasures – playing with her corgis, riding, walking and catching up with her friends.

When Elizabeth succeeded to the throne she told the nation: "My heart is too full for me to say more to you today than I shall always work, as my father did throughout his reign, to advance the happiness and prosperity of my peoples, spread as they are all the world over."

And she has worked tirelessly to make good that vow, attending thousands of engagements both at home and abroad – including

370 last year alone. "You are an anchor for our age," UN General Secretary Ban Ki-moon once told her.

Always welcoming, the Queen is also straight-talking and blunt. During a 2009 photocall with world leaders to mark the G20 summit, she was not amused when Italian Prime Minister Berlusconi bellowed "Mr Obama!" at the US President. She exclaimed: "Why does he have to shout?"

Neither is she immune to life's more frivolous pleasures.

She enjoys a glass of gin and Dubonnet, has been known to browse the Clarins make-up counter at airports, and always carries a lipstick – to discreetly reapply it during official visits.

She has even been known to go night clubbing – she was spotted at Annabel's in Mayfair at the 70th birthday of a senior lady-in-waiting, the Countess of Airlie.

The main Jubilee celebrations will begin in June 2012.

Naturally she will be the centre of our attention, but she is also saying 'Thank You' to us for supporting her for the past half century.

As one of her senior aides said recently: "When you're happy and grateful, what do you do? You give a party and invite friends."

So let us all celebrate a Diamond Jubilee which allows us to be proud to be British.

Inspecting the 2nd Battalion Scots Guards on arrival at the City Chambers, Glasgow, on the third day of her Coronation visit in 1953. Below, on the throne beside her husband Prince Philip at the State Opening of Parliament in the House of Lords, 1999

HIDE AND SEEK

Sheltering from the rain at the official opening of the Lawn Tennis Association's training facility in Roehampton

Queen Elizabeth and King George VI with Princess Elizabeth, aged 18 in 1944. Below, with her father in 1928

IN MEMORY OF 'PAPA'

For the Queen, February 6 denotes the very beginning of her reign and a great sadness at the death of her beloved "Papa".

ALTHOUGH he faced several years of worsening health, including lung cancer, George VI died unexpectedly in his sleep at Sandringham in 1952. Close to her father as a child, Elizabeth was said to be similar to him in character and, according to royal author Sarah Bradford, they shared a "dedicated professionalism".

When the king died, Princess Elizabeth was thousands of miles away in Kenya, watching big game in the Treetops Hotel with the Duke of Edinburgh, unaware of the momentous duty that had fallen upon her shoulders. They were resting after returning to the Sagana Lodge which had been given to them as a wedding present by the people of Kenya, when the message was given to Philip by his equerry and friend Mike Parker. The Duke looked as if half the world had been dropped on him, his close aide once said. Philip broke the sad news to his wife while they were alone. Lady-in-waiting Pamela Mountbatten gave her a hug when she came back inside.

Journalist John Hartley was at the exclusive Treetops Hotel where the then-princess heard the news.

Mr Hartley recalls Lady Pamela said: "I'm so sorry," and the Queen replied, "It's one of those things."

He said: "The Queen maintained rigid self-control, until they were in the plane flying back to London. Then she broke down. After all, it was her father and she was absolutely devoted to him."

Princess Elizabeth, now Queen, was ready to fulfil her duty.

Lord Charteris, her then-private secretary, remembered seeing her seated at her desk in the Lodge appearing "very composed, absolute master of her fate". Asked what name she wished to use as Queen, she is said to have replied simply: "My own name, of course."

The remainder of the Commonwealth tour was immediately cancelled and swift arrangements were made for their return home.

After a long plane journey, the young Queen, a slim, pale figure, dressed in mourning black, made her way down the steps, ahead of the Duke of Edinburgh, and set foot on British soil on February 7 for the first time as the Sovereign. Prime Minister Winston Churchill was the first to greet her, on the runway at London Airport.

Elizabeth had left as a Princess and returned as a Queen at the age of just 25.

The Daily Mirror reported on February 7, 1952, on 'THE YOUNG MOTHER WHO IS NOW QUEEN'.

"At 25 she has become one of the most important people in the world – as the great and symbolic head of the British Commonwealth. The kind of woman she is has therefore become a matter of great moment. One thing is certain. She is a young woman of character.

"But now there faces her a tremendous responsibility. She has become vital because the Commonwealth is an enormously important factor in world affairs and because she has now become for the world a touchstone for Royalty. And Royalty in the Commonwealth is the symbol of the unity of a family. Is there any symbol that could be as powerful?

"How will our Queen Elizabeth II measure up to these demands? The signs are that she will measure up to them very well, even though she is, as people say, 'only 25'. It does not seem very long ago since the two Princesses, with their little dogs, or their ponies, and their model house, and their pantomime pranks, and their Girl Guiding and their tousled hair and wide eyes, were the sweethearts of a nation,

Daily Mirror

THURS FEB. 7 1952

FORWARD WITH THE PEOPLE

at G.P.O. as a Newspaper.

millions saw him

HIS VALET FOUND THE KING DEAD

He called softly to his master—but there was no answer

By 'DAILY MIRROR' REPORTERS

IN a dramatic homeward dash to her sorrowing people, Queen Elizabeth the Second—as she was proclaimed yesterday—was last night flying through the darkness with her consort.

A tropical thunderstorm and heavy rain held up their Argonaut plane at Entebbe Airport, in Uganda, for two and a half hours.

Only a few hours earlier the news of her father's death had been brought to Elizabeth at the Royal Lodge, Nyeri.

It was Mr. Jimmy Macdonald, a personal valet, who found the King dead when he took early morning tea to the Royal bedroom at Sandringham House.

It was as sudden as that.

Mr. Macdonald, a personal valet for many years, thought the King was sleeping. He called him softly. The King, normally a light sleeper, did not reply.

They Called the Queen

Court officials were called from their beds. They hurried in dressing gowns to the Royal Family's personal apartment. The King was dead.

Officials hurried to the bedchambers of the personal staff of the Queen—now the Queen Mother. It was they who summoned Her Majesty to the King's bedroom, where she was joined within a few moments by Princess Margaret.

Soon the whole household was awakened. The Queen was in tears. It was only a few hours that changed the atmosphere of Sandringham House from happiness to tragedy.

For all Tuesday the King was out with his neighbour, Lord Fermoy, shooting on the estate.

The King went out after breakfast at 8.40, lunched at the Flitcham village hall, and did not return to Sandringham until dusk. It was a dry day, and the King bagged nine hares.

While the King was *Continued on Back Page*

A few hours before . . .

Only a few hours before the news of her father's death reached Kenya, this picture of a happy, smiling Princess was taken.

Now, a grief-stricken Queen, she is on her way home.

...PER TURNED HER ...HTER INTO TEARS

...CORRESPONDENT   Nairobi (Kenya), Wednesday.

...of sorrow entered a sunlit room in Royal Lodge, Nyeri, today. Princess Elizabeth ...just a week ago when, despite the bitter ...the Duke of Edinburgh, gaily turned to greet him. Their laughter stopped ...staying his young wife with one hand, moved towards the sad-faced man—the ...retary, Lieutenant-Colonel Martin Charteris.

The colonel whispered to the

...to the Princess, ...y lost its colour. ...her whisper, he ...as passed away ...

...ess stood quite ...face, she burst ...

...er away to her ...that had been ...

...ole and con- ...her return to ...d the legion of ...

Continued on Back Page

The lying in State

THE King, it is expected, will lie in State in Westminster Hall for four or five days. The Duke of Edinburgh, the Duke of Gloucester and Earl Mountbatten will be among those who will mount the Guard of Honour at the bier.

● The King's body will be brought to London before the week-end and final arrangements for the funeral in St. George's Chapel, Windsor Castle, will be made today.

● Queen Elizabeth the Second was Proclaimed Queen last night at an Accession Council in St. James's Palace.

● The Coronation of the new Queen is not expected to take place before the middle of 1952.

● Mr. Churchill will broadcast to the nation at 9.15 tonight. Last night he asked people not to gather at London Airport for the arrival of the Queen.

---

an empire and a world. Two little girls in blue and one of them a Queen in the making. Their memories of bucket and spade on the sands at Bognor Regis with George V – 'Grandpa England' – during his convalescence in 1929. She was Lillibet to him.

"She'll remember the discipline she got from her grandparents.

"She sometimes needed it. In skirmishes with her sister, 'Lillibet was quick with her left hook'. Elizabeth was kept out of the limelight until she was eighteen. The piano lessons at the Palace, the swimming and the dancing and the headstrong spirit that led her to head a Conga parade through the State Chambers are now part of a schooling which was shed as a snake sloughs its skin.

"But at 18 she definitely came out into the kind of life she knew would be hers since they told her, as a ten-year-old tomboy schoolgirl, that one day she would almost certainly be a Queen of England. The teenage study of constitutional history and international affairs, the discipline, work and play had prepared her for this.

"The girl with a will of her own has brought that will to the heart of the Empire. People have seen how much nerve and backbone can stiffen that 5ft 4in figure and have said: 'She has a lot of her grandmother in her.' And a lot of her mother too.

"It won't be her theoretical power which will make her a great Queen – the power to dissolve parliaments, choose Prime Ministers, and unseat them, force elections and the rest. It will be just her Queenly presence, a symbol of national unity, a rallying point of Empire and of decent feelings and behaviour everywhere. Decent behaviour, home ideals, moral values – from now these will be mirrored in the life of one woman. She can look forward to a long reign.

"With the years will come experience and wisdom which will be at the service of her ministers, statesmen and people. In these, more than in the pomp of Royalty, is its power."

On February 8, 1952, Elizabeth II was formally proclaimed Queen at a meeting of the Accession Council in St James's Palace.

The new Queen steps from her plane at London Airport after being recalled from Kenya following the death of her father in 1952

FAMILY TRADITION

King George and family take a Royal tour and inspection of crops at Sandringham, Norfolk, in 1943.
Right, Princess Anne, daughter of Princess Elizabeth and the Duke of Edinburgh is christened at Buckingham Palace in 1950, with Queen Mary, Queen Elizabeth (holding Prince Charles) and the King

King George VI and Queen Elizabeth on the deck of HMS Vanguard with Princesses Elizabeth and Margaret in 1947

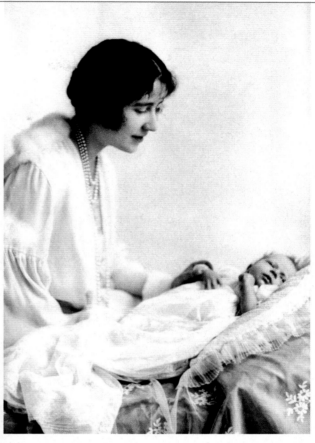

Two sisters join the family on the balcony of Buckingham Palace, after the Coronation of King George VI in 1937

Queen Elizabeth with her daughter Princess Elizabeth in 1926 (above). The future Queen looks nervous in the Royal Box at the Aldershot Tattoo in 1938, aged twelve

Young Elizabeth rides in a horse drawn carriage with her grandparents King George V and Queen Mary in 1931

Top, Princess Elizabeth conducts an inspection of the guard in Albert Square Manchester, in 1949. Above, all smiles at Badminton Horse Trials, with the Duke of Edinburgh and Princess Margaret, a month before the Coronation in 1953. Left, Queen Elizabeth II and Prince Philip with their daughter Princess Anne after her christening ceremony in 1950

Learning basic car maintenance as a Second Subaltern in the Auxiliary Territorial Service, and, below, as Junior Commander in the ATS, inspecting the Motor Transport Training Centre at Camberley, 1945

Girl Guides Elizabeth and Margaret about to send a message by carrier pigeon to Guide Headquarters in 1943. Right, Princess Elizabeth dances arms linked with Lady Pamela Mountbatten during an eightsome reel at The Saddle Club Dance, Malta, in the 1940s

BRIGHT FUTURE

Princess Elizabeth and Prince Philip with their children, Prince Charles and Princess Anne in 1951. One year later, and she would be Queen of England

CROWNING GLORY

The Voice of Britain rang out proudly through the world, raised in triumphant song, as Queen Elizabeth was crowned in Westminster Abbey on June 2, 1953.

The Royal Family on the balcony at Buckingham Palace after the Coronation at Westminster Abbey

IN robes decorated with a repeating pattern of the Tudor rose of England, Elizabeth II took the Coronation Oath to serve her people and maintain the laws of God and was handed the four symbols of authority – the orb, sceptre, rod of mercy and Royal ring of sapphire and rubies.

As the Archbishop of Canterbury placed St Edward's Crown atop her brown hair, the congregation cried out: "God save the Queen!" and a gun salute began.

The Daily Mirror reported: "THE MULITUDE SANG, THE TRUMPETS SOUNDED – THE QUEEN WAS CROWNED.

"Never in all its history has London seen such a sight. The greatest city in the world was crowned with gold and paved with happy faces.

"For at that moment when Queen Elizabeth II was crowned, and the trumpets blared and the nation's voice rose, the people of this land suddenly knew in their hearts that a new era had come.

"All through the land it happened in a flash. A new Golden Age had begun."

As the Queen and Duke of Edinburgh settled into the State coach, "It was a moment of the purest joy as they began the six-mile-long drive back to the palace. Up, up, up rose the thousand upon thousandfold cheers. The vision of the young Queen, radiantly beautiful, was a magic moment that none who saw her will ever forget.

"Then the Queen, still wearing her crown, and with the Duke of Edinburgh and Prince Charles and Princess Anne came on to the palace balcony to watch the RAF fly-past. When night came after the day's pageantry, celebration parties, ox-roasting festivities and firework galas went on all over an exultant, joyous Britain."

Broadcasting to Britain and the world, the Queen summed up her Coronation in these words:

"I am sure that this, my Coronation, is not the symbol of a power and splendour that are gone, but a declaration of our hopes for the future, and for the years I may, by God's grace for mercy, be given to reign and serve you as your Queen.

"Throughout this memorable day I have been uplifted and sustained by the knowledge that your thoughts and prayers are with me. Many thousands of you came from all parts of the Commonwealth and Empire to join in the ceremony.

"But I have been conscious, too, of the millions of others who have shared in it by means of wireless or television in their homes.

"All of you near or far have been united in one purpose. It is hard for me to find words in which to tell you of the strength which this knowledge has given me. The ceremonies you have seen today are ancient and some of their origins are veiled in the mists of the past.

"But their spirit and meaning shine through the ages, never, perhaps, more brightly than now.

"Throughout all of my life and with all of my heart I shall strive to be worthy of your trust."

The Queen ended her message: "As this day draws to its close, I know that my abiding memory will be not only the solemnity and beauty of the ceremony but the inspiration of your loyalty and affection. I thank you all from a full heart. God bless you all."

By night time, the celebrations were drawing to an end, but Elizabeth II's reign was only just beginning. Before the new Queen, the rigours of office. The profound ceremonies of the Coronation, a lengthy tour of the Commonwealth, a first Christmas message which found her racked with nerves. But she did not face it alone.

With her husband's quick wit and remorseless energy to help her, England's second Elizabeth took on the stern business of monarchy with determination.

JOYOUS BRITAIN

The golden state coach procession makes its way back to Buckingham Palace following the Coronation ceremony. Top, Queen Elizabeth II and the Duke of Edinburgh are driven to the Guildhall Square in London for a Coronation banquet – June 12, 1953

Daily Mirror

ORWARD WITH THE PEOPLE

,412 + + + Wednesday, June 3, 1953

CORONATION SOUVENIR

HAPPY

...And this was the happiest picture of all

—AND

Daily Mirror

1½ **FORWARD WITH THE PEOPLE**

No. 15,412 + + Wednesday, June 3, 1953

CORONATION SOUVENI

HAPPY

This was the happiest picture of all

—AND GLORIOUS

MAGIC MOMENT

The Queen and Prince Philip inside the royal carriage during the Coronation procession, June 2, 1953. The Daily Mirror celebrated the occasion and happiness of the nation with special edition souvenir newspapers

Even the British weather couldn't put a damper on the occasion – like thousands of others already on the pavements between Buckingham Palace and Westminster, a crowd of people waited on The Mall for an all-night vigil for the Coronation procession. Below, crowds in Trafalgar Square watch as Troops march past on the return from Westminster Abbey after the Queen's crowning

The women of Pine street in Newcastle make a clean sweep in preparation for their street party in 1953. Right, children in St Paul's Road, Islington, made decorations and flags for the big day

Queen Elizabeth II in her Coronation robes photographed with her family and other members of the Royal Family, in the Throne Room at Buckingham Palace

WIFE, MOTHER & MONARCH

The memories are fresh. Laughter, children at play, pride in achievement. But familes – even Royal ones – have a way of growing on you.

IN 1947, when Princess Elizabeth married, you could have driven a ceremonial coach and horse between the Royal family as they stood on the palace balcony.

In a modern photograph of the Royal family, you can barely see the balcony for relatives. But the Royals, with every addition, represent for us all the strength of family life. And for the Queen, surely, it must reflect the success of her own marriage and her reign.

The Queen's sense of duty dominates everything. People were surprised when she started her 'second family' with the birth of Prince Andrew in 1960 – Charles and Anne were already eleven and nine.

More significant was the fact she had delayed by a decade the creation of the large family she had always wanted, in order to carry out the duties thrust unexpectedly on her by the early death of her father and her own accession.

As a Princess, Elizabeth told a friend before her marriage that she and her husband wanted four children.

But of course, it was the birth of the first that was awaited most eagerly. Crowds waited in the Mall, singing in the damp November air. The controller of the Trafalgar Square fountains waited to hear

A family gathering at Windsor Castle in 1968

whether he should turn the jets of water pink or blue. Charles was born at 9:14 on the evening of November 14, 1948. When Philip was told, he said: "Thank God" and opened the champagne. In 1950 Princess Anne was born. Ten years later

Prince Andrew was born and in 1964, Prince Edward. The new Royal Family was complete.

Lord Louis Mountbatten – or Dickie to a flotilla of intimate friends, revealed in a rare interview before his death, what he

Left, Princess Anne playfully places a daffodil on Prince Edward's head, 1960. Above, the Queen out riding with Prince Edward and Sarah Ferguson in 1988. Below, Peter Phillips, son of Princess Anne, takes a tumble at a family gathering in 1979

thought about the Queen — the lady he called "Betty".

"I've known her ever since she was a small child. I've watched her grow up. To me she is a marvellous person. I have never known her say an unkind or unpleasant thing about anybody. I've never known her entertain a mean or hurtful thought. And I have never known her to be deflected from her sole concerns — the country and her family.

"Let's take her family life. It is really very, very simple. She is head over heels in love with Philip. And he is just as fond of her. The children are devoted to them and each other. Theirs is the very essence of a happy family life."

Prince Andrew speaks fondly of growing up at Windsor Castle and Balmoral and tells how the Queen made "huge sacrifices" to spend time with her four youngsters.

The Duke of York said: "I remember my mother would look after Edward and me ➤

"Don't make me laugh, Grandma!" Prince Harry grins at the Queen as she inspects the Sovereign's Parade at the Royal Military Academy in Sandhurst in 2006

in the evenings in the palace, alone, quite happily. It was a proper family."

He recalled how he and Prince Edward would zoom around state rooms on rollerblades, then sit and watch 'Doctor Who' with their mum. Occasionally, they would come a cropper and she would pick them up saying, just like any other mum: "Don't be so silly, there's nothing wrong with you – just go and clean yourselves up."

Prince Andrew revealed: "My childhood was somewhat military. Things always turned up on time and I remember well that if I didn't turn up to breakfast within five minutes of the appointed time there would be none. My father always dispensed incredibly profound and sound advice. I appreciated that, although I did not always agree with the advice.

"I was brought up at a time when a PDA (public display of affection) was somewhat frowned upon. Remember, it is difficult if you are wearing an Ascot hat or uniform and are on parade. It is then that you whisper, 'Hey, how about later?' and then once you come off parade you give them a jolly good hug." ➤

The Princess of Wales introduces Prince William to the family for the first time in 1982

MUM'S THE WORD

Clockwise from top;
Prince Andrew with the
Queen at Badminton
Horse Trials in 1977;
the Queen and family at
Windsor castle in 1968
– Prince Philip, Prince
Charles, Andrew, Edward
and Princess Anne;
The Queen chats with polo-
playing Prince Philip at
Windsor Great Park, 1956;
Prince Charles keeps
watch on his fourth
birthday in 1952

Queen Elizabeth II and the Duke of Edinburgh gather for a flypast on the balcony of Buckingham Palace, alongside other members of the Royal Family (from left) Princess Eugenie, Princess Beatrice, Prince William, Earl and Countess of Wessex, Prince and Princess Michael of Kent, the Duke of York, The Duchess of Cornwall and the Prince of Wales, 2010

He added: "She is consistent – she has always been there."

Speaking in 1997, on the occasion of their Golden Wedding Anniversary, Prince Philip paid tribute to their children: "Like all families, we went through the full range of the pleasure and tribulations of bringing up children. I am, naturally, somewhat biased, but I think our children have all done rather well under very difficult and demanding circumstances and I hope I can be forgiven for feeling proud of them."

Friends and relatives of the Queen speak of her softer side as well – of a woman who puts duty first but one who also knows when a more personal approach is needed.

She insisted that Prince William wear his Irish Guards colonel uniform when he married Kate because it's the uniform of his most senior military appointment.

But when it came to the guest list, she told her grandson: "Start with your friends first and then go from there."

So, on her instruction, William binned the list of 777 dignitaries that palace officials had given to him.

Many were eventually invited – but only after William had made room for his nearest and dearest. Since the death of the Queen Mum in March 2002, the Queen has also begun to modernise the monarchy in ways which would have been abhorrent to her very traditional mother – such as by allowing William and Kate to live together before their wedding.

Her grandchildren have brought her great joy and with the addition of Savannah Phillips, born to Peter and Autumn Phillips in 2010, Her Majesty celebrated her role as a proud great-grandmother.

QUEEN & CASTLE

Her Majesty with Prince Philip, Princess Anne and Prince Charles at Windsor Castle, 1950.
Below, holding Prince Edward in her arms on the Palace balcony during the the Trooping of the Colour ceremony in 1964

The Queen shares a joke with the Prince of Wales, attending the Braemar Highland Games in 2006

PORTRAIT OF CHANGE

The Royal Family at Buckingham Palace in 1972. Left to right: Prince Charles, Prince Edward, Queen Elizabeth II, the Duke of Edinburgh, Prince Andrew, and Princess Anne. Pictured left, the Queen with grandsons Prince William and Harry at Windsor Great Park in 1987, and below, watching a firework display on her 80th birthday as four of her granchildren giggle behind her – Prince William, Peter Phillips, Zara Phillips and Prince Harry, in 2006

Prince
and Lieut
Mountba
Clyde
launching
RMS Caro
stopped by
Hall to receiv
wedding p
electric sew

MY HUSBAND AND I

In 2012 the Queen and Prince Philip will celebrate 65 years as husband and wife. And it isn't a day too long for them.

Young love – the happy couple in Kenya; pictured left, it's all in the eyes at a gala performance in London, 1952

THEY'VE had their ups and downs, but the Royal couple have rarely been apart since the big day in 1947.

Her Majesty's former private secretary, Lord Charteris, once noted: "Prince Philip is the only man in the world who treats the Queen simply as another human being. He's the only man who can. Strange as it may seem, I believe she values that.

"And, of course, it's not unknown for the Queen to tell Prince Philip to shut up. Because she is Queen, that's not something she can easily say to anybody else."

But the Queen adores him and defers to him. Perhaps it is understandable. Philip knelt before her at her Coronation in 1953 and promised to be her "liege man of life and limb" and that he would "live and die for her". And he has stood by those vows, making him the longest-serving Royal Consort in British history.

It was in 1939, shortly before he went off to war, that Philip and Elizabeth had their first meeting. She was just 13 and he was a promising cadet at Dartmouth Naval College.

They sealed their friendship over ginger biscuits and lemonade, then Philip demonstrated his athleticism by jumping over the nets of the college tennis courts. They kept in touch intermittently – he fought in the Second World ➤

TWO HEARTS

Square dancing at a cowboy fancy dress party during the royal tour of Canada in 1950. Below, wearing Maori Kahu-Kiwi (Kiwi feather cloaks) at Rugby Park in Gisborne, New Zealand during the Silver Jubilee Tour of 1977

Love is in the air on a State visit to Nigeria, in 1959. Above, during their traditional summer break at Balmoral Castle, 1976

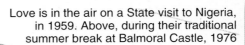

Coast to coast – the couple
relaxing on board a private jet

War before they were ultimately reunited and were married in 1947, spending the first years of married life living in idyllic bliss in Malta.

But any chance of living a peaceful life before Elizabeth would take over the throne were dashed when her father, King George VI, died at the age of just 56. For Philip, there was no question of not taking up his duties as consort, even if it meant putting his own career aspirations on hold.

During a speech on the occasion of their Golden Wedding anniversary in 1997, the Duke of Edinburgh revealed: "The war in the Far East only came to an end late in 1945.

"I got back to this country from the Pacific in January 1946 and in the autumn of 1947 we got married. It was a fairly drab world – the post-war recovery had hardly begun and practically everything was rationed.

"Everyone seemed to think that our wedding was a very happy occasion and brought a little colour back to life after the

dreary war years. At any rate, we certainly thought so."

The Duke recalled that the couple were then fortunate enough to enjoy "five happy years of fairly conventional married life" including two years with the Royal Navy in Malta.

He said: "This period came to an abrupt end when the Queen had the melancholy duty of succeeding her father after his premature death in 1952. She was 25 and I was 30, and we had two small children.

"Life changed dramatically in many ways, but it had much less effect on our married life than I anticipated.

"After an interval of 10 hectic years, we had two more children and were more or less settled into our new way of life. We would both like to acknowledge that it was only through the kindness and consideration of so many people in all walks of life that we managed to get through those early daunting years of added responsibilities."

The Duke saluted the Queen for her tolerance when the going got tough.

And he raised a laugh as he put their successful partnership down to his wife:

"I think the main thing we have learnt is that tolerance is the one essential ingredient of any happy marriage. It may not be quite so important when things are going well, but it is absolutely vital when the going gets difficult.

"You can take it from me that the Queen has the quality of tolerance in abundance.

"I am sufficiently old-fashioned to believe that a great deal more can be achieved by a partnership in marriage. It has been a challenge for us but by trial and experience I believe we have achieved a sensible division of labour and a good balance between our individual and joint interests."

"He has, quite simply, been my strength and stay all these years," said the Queen. "And I, and his whole family, and this and many other countries, owe him a debt greater than he would ever claim or we shall ever know."

SIDE BY SIDE

Arriving at Romsey Abbey for a Royal wedding in 1946 – King George VI, Queen Elizabeth, Princess Elizabeth, Princess Margaret and Lieutenant Philip Mountbatten. Below, Queen Elizabeth and Prince Philip at the Great Wall of China in 1986. Right, holding their first child, Prince Charles, in 1949

Queen Elizabeth II and the Duke of
Edinburgh at Windsor in 1959, joined
by Sugar, one of the Royal corgis

A SILVER
CELEBRATION

The Queen's 1977 Silver Jubilee saw millions of her subjects celebrating at street parties throughout the country, as regal popularity hit a new high.

Two young men have the Queen rocking with laughter at St Katherine's Dock

THE affection shown by crowds of people who turned out to see her during the Jubilee tours of the UK was a surprise even to the Queen.

"I am simply amazed. I had no idea," a lady-in-waiting recalled Her Majesty saying over and over during her visits.

Though the Accession took place in February, the main 25th anniversary celebrations were scheduled for the summer. In February and March, there was an Australasian and Pacific tour, and in October the Queen and Duke of Edinburgh went on a Canadian and Caribbean tour. During the intervening months, there was a build-up of events at home, culminating in the main celebration on June 7. On May 4, the Queen addressed Parliament. Then the United Kingdom tours began, starting in Glasgow.

At the beginning of June there was a London week which climaxed with a river progress up the Thames, fireworks display and a procession of lighted carriages taking the Queen back to Buckingham Palace.

On June 6, the Queen climbed Snow Hill, near Windsor Castle, where – surrounded by thousands of children – she lit a bonfire as the signal for lighting of a hundred other beacons across the country.

Next day, a million people filled The Mall to see the State Coach take the Queen and Prince Philip from the Palace to St Paul's Cathedral, followed by the Prince of Wales on horseback in the scarlet uniform and black bearskin of a Colonel of the Welsh Guards.

After the cathedral service, the Queen and her husband went on a royal walkabout through the City of London, ending at Guildhall where she addressed a luncheon in her honour.

At the beginning of the year, there had been talk of royalty in the doldrums in the wake of the failed marriage of Princess Margaret.

By the autumn, the media reported the monarchy enjoying an exceptional period of popularity and security.

Lord Charteris, the Queen's private secretary, explained: "She had a love affair with the country. Those who accompanied her during the tours came back with a strong sense of the popular emotion – as well as of her own pleasure in the response of the crowds, and their delight in her obvious enjoyment." ➤

MAJESTIC

Laughter at a Government reception in Canberra, during her tour of Australia. Above, the Golden State Coach arrives at St Paul's Cathedral with the Queen and Duke of Edinburgh

REACHING OUT

Visiting the capital of Tonga with the Duke of Edinburgh (above); riding back to the Palace, after lunch at Guildhall, on June 7, 1977 (right); residents of Parry Street, Whitburn, crown Joyce Atchison the Jubilee Queen at a street party (below)

The Daily Mirror reported: "In 1952 the Queen was a slim and pretty young mother of two. Wartime austerity was only gradually receding and Britain still had an Empire.

"In her Silver Jubilee year, the Queen is a trim and well-preserved mother of four. Once again we are having to tighten our belts a bit and 29 British dependencies over which the Queen reigned in 1952 have become independent.

"But as Britain's power in the world has declined the Queen's prestige has risen.

"That is no mean achievement. Britain in the last quarter of the 20th century is slow to tug a traditional forelock and quick to blow a raspberry at any outmoded tradition. The monarchy is a tradition. None more so. But thanks to the Queen it has not become an outmoded one.

"Through her own personal qualities the Queen has adapted tradition to rapidly changing times. Touring frequently, introducing friendly and informal 'walkabouts'. Allowing the TV cameras into the privacy of her home and family life.

"She is liked and admired even by people who would do away with the monarchy altogether. Her reign has coincided with the great march of women's liberation. And the Queen has shown that being a monarch is something a woman can do as well as a man.

"She has proved her worth in many ways. As a world-wide symbol of GREAT Britain. As an export saleswoman supreme. As a lasting example of the strengths of family life.

"No wonder, in this Jubilee Year of 1977, we are all taking our hats off to an outstanding and much-loved Queen."

Pearly Queens June West and Sheila Arrowsmith give a knees up outside Buckingham Palace. Top, the Queen, accompanied by the chairman of Lincoln College Council, during a visit to Christchurch, New Zealand

Children welcoming Queen Elizabeth II as she walks among the crowd on a sports field at Butterley Hall, near Chesterfield, during the Silver Jubilee tour of Great Britain

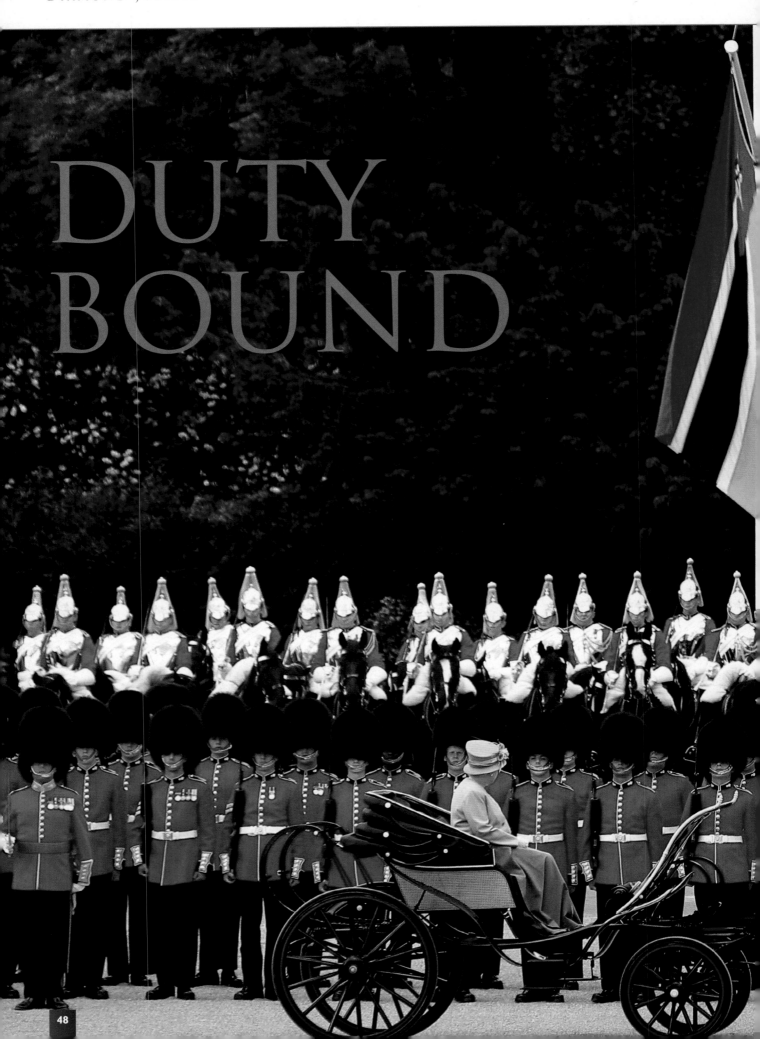

DUTY
BOUND

They call themselves 'The Firm'. The Queen is chairman and around her is the most famous Board of Directors in the world. As Head of State and Head of Nation, Her Majesty leads the Royal family by example.

IT was King George VI who first dubbed his family 'The Firm'. The aim was to work as a close team and to get on with a vital job.

The Queen knows that her business, like any other, has to be accountable – and we, the shareholders, demand good value for money.

In between daily appointments, meetings and matters of State, the Queen manages to fit in a large number of trips around the country for opening ceremonies and meeting the public.

The reaction offered by her staff to anybody who suggests she might be cutting back as she celebrates her 86th birthday this year, is one of laughter, even ridicule. Her work load is still prodigious they say. The Queen remains tireless although her staff will concede that: "we are now pacing the Queen better."

Aptly, with HM's love of horses, this is a racing phrase.

What this means is that instead of travelling on overseas tours for two weeks, such trips are limited to just seven days. Says one of the planners: "We get her in, organise a sensible itinerary and get her out again."

In 2010, at the age of 27, Prince William became a proper paid-up, working member of 'The Firm'. For the first time, his grandmother needed him and asked him to represent her at a major event – travelling to New Zealand to stand in for her at the opening of the Commonwealth country's Supreme Court. ➤

CENTRE STAGE

The Queen inspects soldiers at the Trooping the Colour parade in 2010. Left, a family gathering at the wedding of Princess Anne and Captain Mark Phillips in 1973

William is of course not the only one to support the Queen as she gets older. The rest of the family "muck in". Princess Anne often attends official functions, as do the Prince of Wales, Prince Andrew, Prince Edward, the Gloucesters and Kents. But they do so "in the name of the Queen". For 30 years Prince Charles has stood in for HM at Investitures as has Princess Anne. Even Prince Harry is starting to get more involved as his Diamond Jubilee tour of the Commonwealth nations of Belize, Jamaica and the Bahamas shows.

There are duties only the Sovereign can carry out. Not her husband, Prince Philip; her son and heir Prince Charles or even her grandsons. These include:

- The Cenotaph annual Remembrance Sunday service
- The Trooping the Colour ceremony
- The Garter Ceremony at Windsor Castle
- Commonwealth Heads of Government Meetings
- Weekly meeting with the Prime Minister
- The annual Christmas message
- The annual State Opening of Parliament
- The Queen's distribution of Maundy money

The pageantry and splendour of the Trooping the Colour parade is enjoyed by millions of people worldwide and dates back to 1748, when it was first created to celebrate the birthday of King George II. Although the Queen's actual birthday is April 21, the Trooping the Colour has traditionally been held in June in what has become the Sovereign's "official" birthday.

The Queen prefers a more "low-key", personal birthday.

It is marked by a 41-gun royal salute by the King's Troop Royal Horse Artillery in London's Hyde Park and a 62-gun salute by the Honourable Artillery Company at the Tower of London. The Union Flag is flown on Government buildings.

In 2006, Her Majesty celebrated her 80th birthday, receiving more than 20,000 cards and 17,000 emails from well-wishers in Britain and around the world. She kept up her Royal duties with a visit to Broadcasting House in London to mark the 80th anniversary of the BBC's Royal Charter.

When she was asked what she would like for her birthday, Her Majesty replied: "I don't think there's anything I'd like. A nice sunshiny day – that would be nice."

SUPER TROOPER

Left, Princess Elizabeth, deputising for the King at the Trooping the Colour ceremony for the first time in 1951, leads the mounted procession down the Mall, back to Buckingham Palace. Above, the Queen rides confidently ahead of the parade in the 1960s

CELEBRATIONS

The Queen and the Duke of Edinburgh, followed by the Queen Mother and Prince Charles, at the Garter Ceremony in Windsor, 1975. Right, all smiles on the Queen's 80th birthday in 2006. Below, applause during the Trooping the Colour fly-past in June 1993

Clockwise from left: Her Majesty the Queen during the annual Garter ceremony at Windsor Castle in 1998; a lone figure in black, the Queen places her wreath on the Cenotaph in 1955 when she leads the nation's homage to the dead of two World Wars; presenting Maundy Money in Westminster Abbey in 1981; Queen Elizabeth II bestows the accolade of knighthood on Sir Garfield Barwich QC, at an investiture at Government House, Sydney, in 1955

A LADY OF
LEISURE

Away from the pomp and the pageantry, the private life
of the Queen and Prince Philip is refreshingly ordinary.

The Queen in her
sitting room at
Windsor Castle
in 1977

At work, seated at her desk in Buckingham Palace in 1959. The Queen is seen opening one of the 'boxes' in which documents and papers, sorted for her attention, are sent upstairs by the Private Secretary. Behind the Queen is the Palace switchboard

HER Majesty may have reigned for 60 years, but we hardly know the Queen and her husband at all. Their life inside Buckingham Palace, in the heart of our largest city, remains largely a subject of conjecture and rumour.

But inside reports reveal a Royal couple with fascinatingly ordinary foibles, interests, likes and dislikes. Their day begins at around 8:15 when pages wake them with a cup of tea. Valets prepare and run baths. A big hot breakfast will be placed on hotplates and the morning papers laid out. 'The Sporting Life' is the Queen's favourite read.

She scrutinises its racing gossip, news and selections while Prince Philip buries his nose in the Financial Times. They also read the other papers, particularly when they are in them. The Queen is fond of horoscopes — although she likes it to be understood that she does not really believe them, they are simply an 'amusing diversion'.

The Queen has reduced grand old Buckingham Palace, with its miles of carpeted corridors, to the proportions of an ordinary middle-class home in which, on occasion,

the television dominates the proceedings. This is a source of anxiety to footmen, for the Royal pair have been known to become so engrossed in a programme that they have forgotten there are staff there waiting to clear away and serve the next course.

The Queen likes her evening meal at 8:15; lunch at 1:15 — she appears to have a thing about meals commencing 15 minutes after the hour and they are served by a couple of footmen watched over by a page.

She enjoys a gin and tonic before dinner and a little wine with the meal. Prince Philip prefers dry martinis or the occasional Scotch.

Although it is simply "the office" for the Queen and the Duke, Buckingham Palace is a haven of security in a rough old world for many of their servants.

No new member of the staff is ever presented or shown to the Queen. But she is informed about the new arrival and will watch keenly, if unobtrusively, as he goes about his tasks.

Those she chooses as footmen and pages are selected purely on the impression they make on her. Obviously, dog lovers — and

that even rarer breed, corgi fans — have a head start.

The corgis are the Queen's constant companions and she is devoted to them. She defleas them, takes them for long walks and even lets them sleep in her bedroom. It is hardly a dog's life, in the Royal palaces. The corgis should know better than to bite the hand that feeds them, but from time to time, Her Majesty has been known to have a nip from her favourite four-legged friends.

In March 1991, the Queen was forced to conduct an investiture with her left hand bandaged and her thumb and forefinger sporting plasters, after "she was bitten by one of her corgis when she waded in to stop a dust-up among the snarling dogs", revealed The Mirror newspaper.

"One of her first pets, Susan — given to her on her 18th birthday — started the tradition that Royal corgi tempers are as short as their little legs", it was reported. "Susan had teeth like a crocodile, according to one limping policeman.

"Her favourite target was the ankles of the Royal clockwinder. Footmen defended ➤

themselves by developing a back flip, giving the little terrors a sly boot. Anyone caught in the act was fired."

Staff find it hard to adjust to the fact that the Queen moves among them in an ordinary, relaxed way. Many Royal servants see the Queen only once a year, when she parades the whole staff and distributes their Christmas presents.

One year, a new member of staff was so overcome by this first, close sighting that he dropped to his knees. "Please do stand up" chuckled the Queen, as two colleagues struggled to raise the most ardent monarchist to his feet.

Although Buckingham Palace is cosy enough, Windsor is their real home in the south. Her Majesty looks her most happy when sloshing around the muddy countryside in wellies, scarf on her head, and dogs tumbling around her feet.

Her second home seems to be at the racetrack — that's when the public can see the uninhibited, exuberant side her friends know so well. The Queen and Queen Mother shared an almost-obsessive love of horse racing and they liked to gossip about the lives of owners, trainers and jockeys.

Her Majesty will jump up and down with excitement at the races when she is urging on one of her own horses. This is one of the rare occasions when she throws her solemn regal composure to the winds. The outside world sees the woman who giggles through party games or joins in parlour sing-songs with her friends. Racing vies her one further satisfaction.

It is a tough fiercely competitive sport and when one of her horses wins, no one can say it was because she is Queen.

Her triumph as an owner.

Walking the corgis on the beach near Sandringham; above, relaxing in the drawing room at Balmoral

The Queen prepares to go for an afternoon drive with her daughter, Princess Anne, from Windsor Castle, in 1959

PAWS FOR THOUGHT

The Queen at play frequently wears casual country clothes and is surrounded by dogs – especially her beloved corgis, taking the reigns here in 1980

Wearing sunglasses, the Queen shares a joke with her racing manager, Captain Charles Moore, on the balcony overlooking the unsaddling enclosure at Goodwood races in 1958. Right, Her Majesty focuses on the action at the Windsor Horse Show in 1976. Below, enjoying the countryside with her dog Wren on Deeside in 1960

PHOTO FINISH

Perhaps Her Majesty was getting her own back on the paparazzi by taking some pictures of her own at the Royal Windsor Horse Trials in 1981. Right, cheering on the winner of the 1978 Derby. Below, reading the tea leaves to predict a Derby Day winner in 1982

The Royal Yacht 'Britannia' and the skyline of Detroit, Michigan, seen during a Royal Tour in 1959

HER HUMAN TOUCH

She is the most famous woman in the world and probably the best-loved as well. In the 60 years since she became Queen, the rather shy young woman has been transformed into a figure unequalled on the world's stage.

The Queen and Duke of Edinburgh meet Jackie Kennedy and President Kennedy at Buckingham Palace in 1961

IN her Jubilee tours this year, the Queen will face unprecedented crowds. But Her Majesty knows that danger is part of the job and that if she were surrounded by too much security it would destroy one essence of her work – contact with ordinary people.

Whenever she goes on tours around the world, letters warn hosts that she prefers not to be flanked by motorcycle outriders. She feels they have unpleasant associations with the 1930s and cut her off too much from the crowds. Her life has been threatened on several occasions.

In 1961, when she was due to visit Ghana, there were fears she might be struck down by a bullet intended for her host, President Nkrumah. There were demonstrations and a bomb explosion and two elder statesmen, Winston Churchill and Anthony Eden warned of the risks. But the Queen insisted she must travel and her tour was a gigantic success.

Harold Macmillan, Prime Minister at the time, wrote in his diary: "The Queen has been absolutely determined all through.

"She is impatient of the attitude towards her to treat her as a WOMAN, and a film star or mascot. She has indeed, the heart and stomach of a man . . . she loves her duty and means to be a queen and not a puppet."

To protect her position as Head of State, not only in Britain but in dozens of countries around the world, the Queen has to make tough decisions. She never flinches. At Commonwealth conferences she will single out warring presidents, take them into a room, sit on a throne if need be, and tell themselves to pull themselves together.

Almost single-handedly she has kept the Commonwealth together through sheer strength of character. Occasionally, heads of state do not treat her with respect. On a State visit to Morocco in 1980, King Hassan decided to play golf instead of officially greeting the Queen. During the return visit to Britain a year or so later, Hassan was the guest of the Queen on the Royal Yacht. After bidding him farewell at the top of the gangway, the King took a few steps and turned to wave.

He found nobody there. Honour had been partially restored. ➤

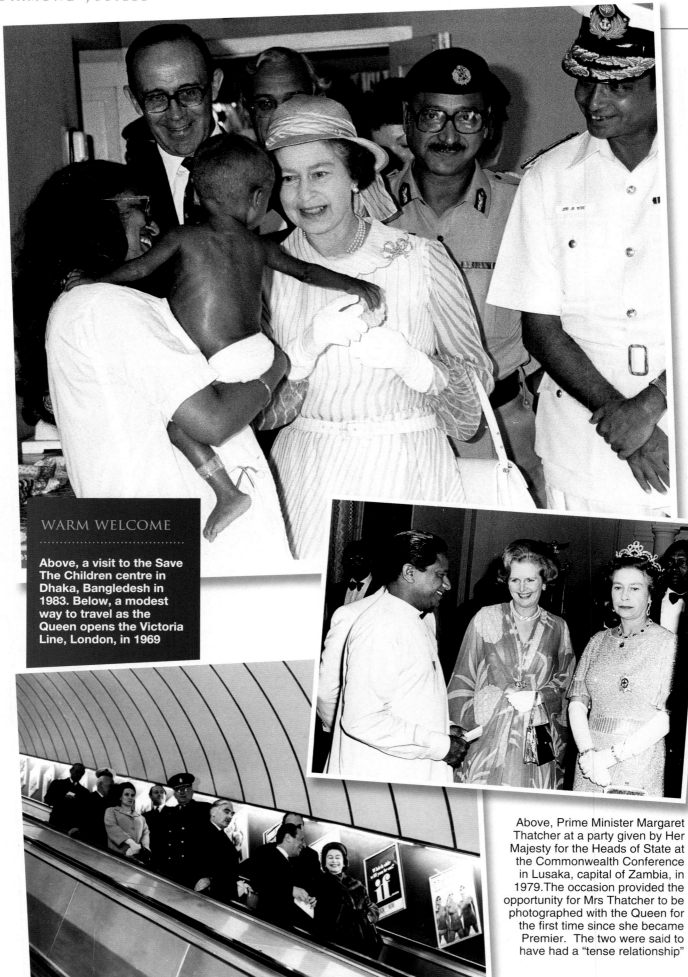

WARM WELCOME

Above, a visit to the Save The Children centre in Dhaka, Bangledesh in 1983. Below, a modest way to travel as the Queen opens the Victoria Line, London, in 1969

Above, Prime Minister Margaret Thatcher at a party given by Her Majesty for the Heads of State at the Commonwealth Conference in Lusaka, capital of Zambia, in 1979.The occasion provided the opportunity for Mrs Thatcher to be photographed with the Queen for the first time since she became Premier. The two were said to have had a "tense relationship"

Marilyn Monroe was among stars who lined up to meet the Queen at the premiere of 'The Battle of the River Plate' in 1956. Left, fashions raise a smile during a Royal visit to Aden in 1954

The Queen's official visits have ranged from the Cocos Islands, 5.4 square miles with a population of 596, to China, 3.7 million square miles with a population of 1.34 billion. Unusual live gifts given to the monarch on foreign tours include: two tortoises presented in the Seychelles in 1972; a seven-year-old bull elephant called Jumbo from the president of Cameroon in 1972 to mark the Queen's silver wedding anniversary; and two black beavers presented after a visit to Canada.

Her gloved hand has been squeezed by rock stars and actors, politicians and presidents, comedians and clergymen, all the high, the good and the great. Movie star Barbra Streisand, dressed in a velvet cloak and hood, sparked controversy at the royal premiere of 'Funny Lady' when she defied convention by speaking first after being introduced to the Queen. She asked why women had to wear gloves when men did not. The Queen was not amused.

While visiting President Bush Senior in 1991, the Queen made a speech at the White House behind a podium that was so high only her hat could be seen. A TV man was heard shouting: "She's gone. All I've got is a talking hat." Her Majesty got her own back for 'podiumgate' during her next speech to Congress when she said: "I hope you can see me from where you are today."

Her Majesty's meeting of the Obamas in 2009 was the most touchy-feely Royal meeting anyone can remember. The Queen and America's First Lady Michelle Obama hugged as stuffy Palace protocol went out of the window. President Barack Obama and his wife gave her an iPod loaded with hits from musicals while the Queen presented them with a framed photograph of herself.

Despite having spent a lifetime meeting strangers, the Queen still cares about the impression she makes. Royal party planner Lady Elizabeth Anson revealed: "People might think she wouldn't have time to worry about menus, tastings and how things look, but she is the most meticulous hostess. She is really interested in what people are going to eat or when they will get drinks."

During her public visits, many wonder about what is euphemistically known as 'the arrangements'. Lord Mountbatten once revealed sensitive intelligence on the matter.

"When she hears that for a special function or Royal Premiere they've repainted the lavatory or put in a new loo in the event that she might use it, the Queen says: 'It is very kind of them, but I never go to the loo'".

And the secret which, well, has been handed down from throne to throne is, "the old rule of never eating or drinking anything for some hours before the event."

Her Majesty keeps her sweetest smile for the children with posies and the grandmothers who offer their hands in friendship. They know how it feels when you have seen so much come and go, the good and the bad, down the years. The new ones see her charm and celebrate what is now. The old ones share history with her. The others just cheer, wave and shout words of encouragement.

Her Majesty is modest — shy, her friends say. But she has a sense of fun. Above all she has dignity. She might be a little unfashionable to some, but rather that than be a phoney. She has always had a timeless and regal elegance. She doesn't need a crown — you can see it in her smile.

HATS OFF

The Queen and Duke of Edinburgh drive through the crowds in a Land Rover at the Bushman's Carnival in Brisbane, during the Royal tour of Australia in 1963

Wearing a cloak of brown kiwi feathers, the Queen meets Maori warriors at Rugby Park, Gisborne, at the opening of the Royal New Zealand Polynesian Festival in 1977

A relaxing way to travel, on board Liverpool's Merseyrail network in 1978

MEET & GREET

Above, the Queen visits Silverwood Colliery, near Rotherham, South Yorkshire in 1975. Right, a meeting of minds at this Manchester school in 1965. Below, Nelson Mandela visits Windsor Castle in 1998. Bottom right, a big thumbs-up for the Royal visit in 1982

What makes the Queen laugh? In this case, it was a cardboard cut-out of DJ Jimmy Saville, during a visit to Fort William in 1991 (above). Left, visiting the home of a war veteran during her Coronation tour of Scotland in 1953

BLOOMING GREAT

Youngsters join the Queen on her 60th birthday in 1986, as she collects daffodils outside the Palace

ICONIC SOUVENIRS

PUBLISHED BY TRINITY MIRROR

WILLS & KATE:
A ROYAL LOVE STORY

Celebrating the romance
between Willliam and Kate

84-page glossy magazine special

Was £4.99
Now Only
£2.00
+ £1 P&P (UK)

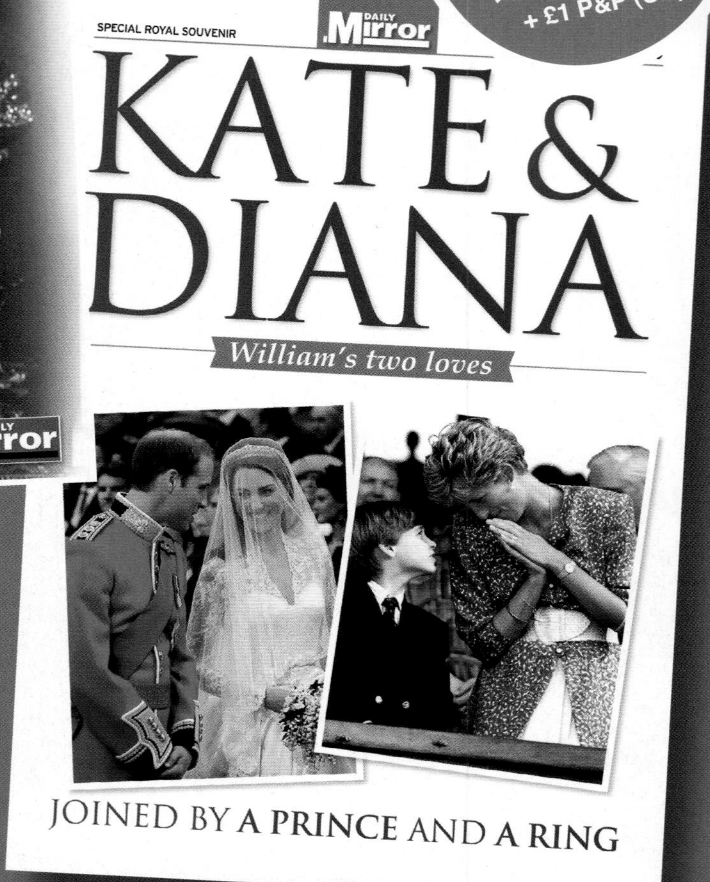

Was £4.99
Now Only
£2.00
+ £1 P&P (UK)

KATE & DIANA
William's two loves –
joined by a Prince and a ring

84-page glossy magazine special

TEARS AMONG THE TRIUMPH

Most people who complete 50 years in a job get a gold watch. The Queen received rather more during her Golden Jubilee in 2002. It was no more than she deserved after a decade of difficult times for the Royal family.

IN 1992 the Queen went through what she memorably called her annus horribilis.

The House of Windsor was dogged by rows between Charles and Diana as they announced their divorce. For the first time the royals received massive hostility following a proposal to make people pay for a fire at Windsor Castle.

An inner strength and resilience saw the Queen cope with her troubles. But three months into 2002 – the year of the Golden Jubilee – and it had become her real annus horribilis.

Despite her knowledge that both Princess Margaret and the Queen Mother were desperately ill and their days numbered, nothing could have prepared the Queen for their deaths coming so close together. Nothing ever could.

Most people in an ordinary family might find it hard to understand just how close-knit this group of women were. But the bond was merely a reflection of the way they were brought up.

Princess Elizabeth and Princess Margaret were unique in a world that was too advanced, way beyond the expectations of their Edwardian parents. ➤

The Queen leaves Westminster Abbey following the funeral of the Queen Mother. Left, Princess Elizabeth, aged 9, with her sister Princess Margaret and Queen Elizabeth the Queen Mother, in 1935

Above, the Queen Mother celebrates her 100th Birthday in August 2000, pictured with the Queen and Princess Margaret. Left, fire rips through Windsor Castle in 1992

Happier times for Prince Charles, Diana and the Queen in 1981, after the couple's engagement; right, the sea of flowers outside the gates of Kensington Palace before the funeral of the Princess of Wales, in 1997

The Queen Mother came from a time when political correctness didn't mean a light and the monarchy existed by a "divine right."

There was no need then to bend in the wind of public opinion or even justify their position in society. Her blissful unawareness of the way the majority of the population lived their lives must have caused the Queen privately to despair. She, after all, has tried at least to keep up with current issues. However, she remains totally supportive, indulgent even, of her mother's idiosyncrasies.

A senior royal source said at the time: "It is a very sad time for the Queen – within two months she has lost her mother and her sister – but she is stoic."

That double sadness brought out the best in the British people. The reaction to the death of the Queen Mother was astonishing.

It was the best Jubilee gift the nation could have given the Queen. She realised how much her mother had been loved. And how important the royal family remains in the life of the country.

When George VI became King, the monarchy faced collapse following the abdication of Edward VII. Elizabeth's father restored dignity and respect to it, especially through his wartime leadership. There were doubts that Queen Elizabeth could carry on what he had achieved. In fact, she did more

than that. But the world was changing and she had to change, too. That is never easy.

She was criticised for not making the Royals more accessible. And when she did, she was criticised for that, too. She shared the joy of every mother when her children married.

And the misery of their marital break-ups. The marriages of three of her four children ended in divorce. The finger of blame was pointed at the Palace, especially over Diana, whose extraordinary popularity threatened the monarchy itself.

When Diana died in 1997 it seemed possible that the monarchy might not survive until the Golden Jubilee. Yet it did.

Jubilant Britain crowned the Queen's Golden Jubilee with a nationwide party that spread across the globe. The celebrations started with the launch of a "musical beacon" of the Beatles' hit 'All You Need is Love'.

Clearly delighted, the Queen and Prince Philip were seen tapping their feet in time to the music. The message was taken up by choirs across the country and reflected in an extraordinary display of public affection as more than 500,000 people took part in at least 5,000 street parties.

Jubilee fever touched patriotic Brits in the most unlikely way in the most unlikely places.

For almost the first time in her life, the Queen got something wrong.

She just wouldn't believe that people would really, really want to celebrate her Golden Jubilee.

But as she stood on her balcony at Buckingham Palace – the scene of so many triumphs and days of celebration in the past 150 years – she looked down on a sea of faces, maybe as many as one million. And all of them were giving the message: "Well done, Ma'am. We think you're great and we want you to go on for ever."

And the Queen's radiant smile went on for ever during the celebrations. It was there at the classical concert in her back garden, at the pop concert, during an extraordinary firework display and then again as she was carried through the city in a wonderfully over-the-top coach (used on her Coronation Day and again when she celebrated her Silver Jubilee.)

It didn't stop there. When the great moment finally came and Her Majesty stepped out on to her balcony to watch her planes pass overhead, there were tears of joy. When the enormous crowd sang 'Land Of Hope And Glory', there were more. They were not just for the country or for this royal milestone, but for her.

After so many troubles and difficulties, she was back in the affections of her people more powerfully than ever.

Golden smile – jubilee fever sweeps the country as thousands flock to the Mall to join in the celebrations

PRIDE OF BRITAIN

Youngsters at Mountcastle Green in Edinburgh go for gold with their street party; the Queen looks delighted as she watches a display on board HMS Ark Royal in Portsmouth. Below, Her Majesty and the Duke of Edinburgh show their appreciation to the crowds outside Buckingham Palace

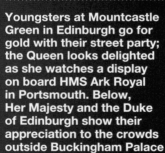

JUBILEE JEWELS

In celebration of the 2012 Diamond Jubilee, here are 60 fascinating facts about our monarch . . .

1 Elizabeth Alexandra Mary Windsor was born at 17 Bruton Street, London, W1, on April 21, 1926, which was then her parents home and is now a Chinese restaurant.

2 Many people sent the then-Princess Elizabeth clothing coupons for her wedding dress during post-war rationing in 1947. She returned the coupons as it was illegal to give them away.

3 The Queen signals to staff with her handbag. If she wants to leave a dinner in five minutes, she puts her bag on the table. She moves it from arm to arm to tell aides she is tired of talking to someone.

4 Her robes were so heavy at her Coronation that she asked the Archbishop of Canterbury to give her a push, saying: "Get me started."

5 Her Majesty went behind the bar of the Queen Vic on a tour of the EastEnders set in 2001.

6 She carries good luck charms from her children in her bag, including miniature dogs and horses and family photos. One picture of Andrew was taken after his safe return from the Falklands.

7 The Queen's favourite television shows include Midsummer Murders, Only Fools and Horses, Doctor Who and The Good Life.

8 The Queen is the second longest serving monarch after Queen Victoria who reigned for 63 years. Only six kings and queens in British history have reigned for 50 years or more – Victoria, Elizabeth II, George III, James VI of Scotland (James I of England), Henry III and Edward III.

9 She is a patron of the Royal Pigeon Racing Association and maintains the Royal Lofts at Sandringham.

10 The Diamond Diadem crown worn by the Queen at the Coronation was made in 1820 for the coronation of King George IV. The design features roses, thistles and shamrocks – the symbols of England, Scotland and Ireland.

11 She has owned more than 30 corgis during her reign. The first, Susan, was an 18th birthday present.

12 A Security guard denied her entry to a private stand at the Royal Windsor Horse Show in 1991. He later said: "I thought she was some old dear who had got lost."

13 Her Majesty has opened Parliament every year except 1959 and 1963, when she was expecting Prince Andrew and Prince Edward respectively.

14 The Queen and Prince Philip joined the 93,000 spectators at Wembley Stadium to watch England win the 1966 World Cup Final.

15 The only year she did not deliver a Christmas message was 1969. She felt the public had seen enough of her in a TV documentary.

16 When Australian Prime Minister Paul Keating broke protocol in 1992 and put his arm around her, he was dubbed "the Lizard of Oz".

17 An avid reader, she loves crime thrillers by PD James, Agatha Christie and Dick Francis.

18 Over her reign the monarch has given regular audiences to 12 prime ministers: (Sir Winston Churchill, Sir Anthony Eden, Harold Macmillan, Sir Alec Douglas-Home, Harold Wilson, Edward Heath, James Callaghan, Margaret Thatcher, John Major, Tony Blair, Gordon Brown, and David Cameron)

19 One of her corgis mated with a dachshund belonging to Princess Margaret to produce a new breed called a dorgi. She now has three dorgis which are called Cider, Candy and Vulcan.

20 The Queen's collections of art, furniture, jewels and horses are thought to be worth around £70 million.

21 Michael Fagan broke into her bedroom at Buckingham Palace in 1982. Reports at the time said that he sat on her bed for 10 minutes as she engaged him in conversation. Fagan says instead that she ran straight out of the room, "her little bare feet running across the floor".

22 She laughed when she shook hands with shot-put champion Geoff Capes at the Braemar Highland Games in 1982 and their hands stuck together because of the resin he used for his grip.

23 Although the Queen is a great dog-lover, she cannot abide cats.

24 The monarch has answered around three and a half million items of correspondence.

25 Balmoral, its castle and 50,000 acres of woods, moors and lochs, and Sandringham Estate – with houses, 60 acres of gardens and 20,000 acres of forest – are all owned by the Queen and worth around £95m.

26 When the Queen and Prince Philip were reunited in Portugal in 1957 after a four-month separation because of official duties, he wore a tie with hearts on.

27 She banks with Coutts & Co and there is a Coutts cash machine at Buckingham Palace.

28 She joined crowds in London to celebrate VE day on May 8, 1945. In her diary she wrote: "Trafalgar Square, Piccadilly, Pall Mall, walked simply miles. Saw parents on balcony at 12.30am – ate, partied, bed 3am!"

29 Since 1952, the Queen has conferred more than 404,500 honours and awards.

30 She performed her first official solo engagement at the age of 17 and was so nervous one of her mother's ladies-in-waiting gave her a barley sugar sweet from her handbag to calm her.

31 The Queen learnt to drive in 1945. Her official car does not need a number plate.

32 Technically, she still owns the sturgeons, whales and dolphins – known as Fishes Royal – in the waters around the UK because of a 1324 statute.

33 Prince Philip's pet names for his wife are said to include "cabbage" and "sausage".

34 When asked what would be discussed with the Queen at their weekly meetings, Churchill would reply: "Racing". Michael Foot would say: "Dogs".

35 Her Majesty has given out approximately 90,000 Christmas puddings to staff, continuing the custom of George V and George VI.

36 As a child, the Queen fell into Buckingham Palace Lake while looking for duck eggs.

37 The Queen unveiled a commemorative statue to comedy legend Eric Morecambe in 1999 – bringing some sunshine to his hometown of Morecambe. The 1977 Christmas special of the Morecambe and Wise show was watched by more people than the Queen's speech and she herself is said to have put the turkey roast back an hour to watch their festivities.

38 During the past 60 years almost one and a half million people have attended garden parties at Buckingham Palace or the Palace of Holyroodhouse. The Queen ended debutante presentation parties in 1958.

39 In November 1944, at Clydebank HMS Vanguard became the first of 23 ships she has launched.

40 The Queen has sat for 129 portraits during her reign.

41 She became the first member of the Royal Family to be awarded a gold disc after 100,000 copies of the CD of the Party at the Palace were sold.

42 When she was four she was given her first horse, a Shetland pony called Peggy, by her grandfather.

43 Her Majesty's jockeys wear purple silks, with scarlet sleeves, gold braiding and a black cap.

44 In her message of congratulations to astronauts after the first moon landing in 1969, she said: "On behalf of the British people I salute the skill and courage which have brought Man to the moon. May this increase the knowledge and well-being of mankind."

45 All her life, the Queen has kept a diary, which has never been seen by anybody else.

46 The 2002 Party at the Palace pop concert was watched by around 200 million viewers worldwide.

47 During the Trooping the Colour ceremony in June 1981, 17-year-old Marcus Serjeant fired six blank cartridges at the Queen before he was subdued. He was charged under the Treason Act and spent three years in custody.

48 The Queen is a patron of more than 620 charities and organisations.

49 The Royal Yacht Britannia was launched in 1953 and decommissioned in 1997, travelling more than a million miles.

50 When the Queen is angry she drums her fingers. When she is very angry she will say: "How amusing for you" and walk away.

51 According to former Royal chef Darren McGrady, who worked for the Queen for 11 years, her beloved corgis are fed "wonderful" food including steak, poached chicken and rabbit.

52 While singing 'Auld Lang Syne' for New Year in 2000, the Queen joined hands with Prime Minister Tony and Cherie Blair and Prince Philip but she got the movements wrong and didn't cross her arms.

53 Elizabeth and Princess Margaret were taken on their first journey on the London Underground railway system by governess Marion Crawford in 1939.

54 Every morning, she starts the day with a cup of tea. The "calling tray" is brought into her bedroom laden with a silver teapot, a water jug and milk . . . as well as a plate of biscuits for her dogs.

55 The Queen has joked that: "We'll go quietly if Britain ever wants to become a Republic."

56 Since 1952 the Queen has given royal assent to more than 3,500 Acts of Parliament.

57 At the beginning of her reign the Queen requested that her husband, rather than her sister, act as regent for a young Prince Charles in the event of her death.

58 There is said to be a Billy Bass singing fish on top of the grand piano at Balmoral.

59 When she met artist Tracey Emin at the Turner Contemporary art centre in Kent in 2011, she asked her: "Do you show internationally as well as in Margate?"

60 The Queen's favourite Blue Peter presenter was John Noakes and she personally requested he attend the BBC children's show's 50th birthday party.

REIGNING SUPREME

After 60 years, the nation will come together in June 2012 to celebrate the Diamond Jubilee of Queen Elizabeth II.

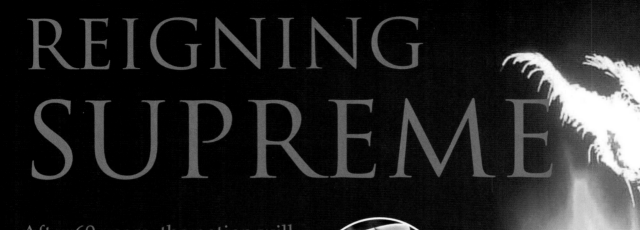

IN the years she has been on the throne, Queen Elizabeth II has achieved much.

If on the day she was crowned the Queen had been asked what she hoped for in 60 years' time, she would almost certainly have said: "To leave the monarchy stronger." She has achieved that.

She has made the monarchy stronger. She has earned and kept the respect of the British people.

And after these Diamond Jubilee celebrations, Elizabeth II will go down in history as one of the United Kingdom's greatest monarchs. She has reigned over us for 60 years. May she and her heirs reign over us for a good many more years.

Queen Elizabeth II smiles with the Duke of Edinburgh on Horse Guards Parade during the annual Trooping the Colour in 2009

A new generation of Royals – Prince William and his wife Kate Middleton, the Duchess of Cambridge, kiss on the balcony of Buckingham Palace, following their wedding at Westminster Abbey in 2011